Wings like Eagles

Mary Kamel

Presentation by *BookLeaf Publishing*

Web: www.bookleafpub.com

E-mail: info@bookleafpub.com

ISBN: 9789357696326

First edition 2023

DEDICATION

To my family and all the wonderful people I
encounter in life who have inspired me

Hills and Valleys

1

The vast green and the broad Blue awakened my soul.

"You will show me the path of life"- Psalm 16

Strength for the weak

My eyelids drooped down,
heavy from the days work.
just like the clouds lining the sky,
grey about to cascade with rain.
"He gives strength to the weak",
it says so in His Word,
I know it too,
His Grace is sufficient,
for through Him we are made new.

Yellow Lady Bug

They call her Yellow Lady Bug,
She runs to her own rhythm,
a smile, sky-wide, on her face.
but, sometimes the words don't come out,
though she has plenty to say.
she makes colourful flower and leaf sandwiches
and says to me 'eat',
I make-believe to eat,
entering her world.
It must be magical in her mind, an imagination
travelling to space,
but it must also be hard to be misunderstood at times,
wanting to play with others who hesitate.
two of her classmates hug her and hold her hand, they
bring her to the line.
She is loved here, and that's reason to celebrate.

Butterfly

Hope landed on the ground next to me,
Flakes of orange and brown lined it's wings.
A sign of all the good things that come to those
who wait.

Horizons

The drive home always eased her mind
as she headed towards the green and the
light-laced clouds.
The wind gushing through the window- a cool
symphony.

"Prayer places our mind in the brilliant radiance
of the Divine light"- St. Francis De Sales

Do not swim

The sign held a "do not swim" symbol, yet
I am here swimming in my thoughts,
praying for the light to enter in and show me the way
of Truth and Wonder, of Hope and Life.

Now

Thoughts swirled around in my head,
yet You are calling me to the: now!
Time is precious says the books,
The old engrave it on the nooks.

Lunar Eclipse

I missed the moon meeting the sun,
but we saw the wild red and orange,
covering the sky,
a time of chasing the light, said I.

A better way

I drove down a windy road,
beautiful farms and pastures surrounding me.
This narrow way I thought,
was not the route I usually take.
A creature of Habit I often go the same way,
but, the GPS re-directed me this time.
The road God leads us down might be longer
and have more turns than we would choose for
ourselves,
but oh how if we trust it will be more beautiful and
better for us
than we expect. And to think I might have missed the
beauty if I chose my own way.

Eyes of the Beloved

10

Seek Understanding,
It expands our vision of Love,
there is not a face you will look into,
that God doesn't Love.

Judy

She sat on a walker by the wayside,
taking in the sun and the cars,
I approached her with a wild flower and a leaf,
she greeted me with a smile and deep gratitude,
the heart of a child. Its funny how age can chisel
away our facade and help us appreciate our being.
I told her how brave I thought she was,
a truth that echoed while I observed her shadow on
the grass.

Brave the Sheep

12

I met a sheep once,
along the Emerald way,
My mum and I named Him Brave,
for he did not flee away.
He stood near us and gave us the gift of presence,
communicating with a "maaay".
I took a picture of his golden eyes,
ones that really saw you,
never mind the hay.

Open doors

13

One closed door,
is a re-direction to another opportunity.

"A man's heart plans his way, but the Lord
directs His steps"
(Proverbs 16:9)

A day to Remember

14

Poppy fields,
silence,
Bugle,
Peace,
Freedom,
Trenches,
The last call,
new life.

Living outside the box

15

Shoes off,
running free.
Puddles,
Climbing Trees.

Dear to Him

My hearts hurts,
But, I need to give my heart,
and my hurt to the One who is greater and above
both.
It is in Him we belong,
that we are valued, that we have dignity.
Not, in how other people treat us.
Fret not, we are dear to Him.

Inquiry

Megalodons in trenches,
do they exist? he asked.
perhaps just in our imagination
like leprechauns,
as he flipped through the book.

Building

Mulching the garden Bed
Labourers busy at work
Rain expectant
But fire burning within,
There is purpose here
A brick atop a brick is the steady way a building gets
built
One hand atop another
The church is mint
It's more than just a building,
It's a house of prayer, it's the people from far and near
through time, and now that bind it together with Her
head being Christ.

Friday Liturgy

His words are a sweet as honey
But they can be sour to the stomach,
Why, said I?
Because they challenge us,
To Forgive, to Love thine Enemy
And to Bless those who curse.

Laughter

They told me knock knock jokes,
they giggled and squirmed in their seats
they loved seeing my reactions
and I loved being kept on my feet.

A New Leaf

Leave a space for God to do something new,
said Henri,
I see the bud, opening, said I,
after the winter the blooms emerge,
just after it seems they are dead.
God gives new life,
in Him there is no dread.